T0067785

# I'm Here with You

Alexander StPaul Lawani

ARCHWAY
PUBLISHING

Copyright © 2022 Alexander StPaul Lawani.

All rights reserved. No part of this book may be used or reproduced by
any means, graphic, electronic, or mechanical, including photocopying,
recording, taping or by any information storage retrieval system
without the written permission of the author except in the case
of brief quotations embodied in critical articles and reviews.

This book is a work of non-fiction. Unless otherwise noted, the author
and the publisher make no explicit guarantees as to the accuracy
of the information contained in this book and in some cases, names
of people and places have been altered to protect their privacy.

Archway Publishing books may be ordered
through booksellers or by contacting:

Archway Publishing
1663 Liberty Drive
Bloomington, IN 47403
www.archwaypublishing.com
844-669-3957

Because of the dynamic nature of the Internet, any web addresses or
links contained in this book may have changed since publication and
may no longer be valid. The views expressed in this work are solely those
of the author and do not necessarily reflect the views of the publisher,
and the publisher hereby disclaims any responsibility for them.

Any people depicted in stock imagery provided by Getty Images are
models, and such images are being used for illustrative purposes only.
Certain stock imagery © Getty Images.

ISBN: 978-1-6657-2648-1 (sc)
ISBN: 978-1-6657-2649-8 (e)

Library of Congress Control Number: 2022912295

Print information available on the last page.

Archway Publishing rev. date: 08/09/2022

# Contents

# Introduction

The poems in this book highlight many different aspects of life experiences, emotions, and psychological difficulties that many people face in life. This book focuses on the experiences and emotions that are often difficult for some to comprehend, let alone make sense of. I wrote this book bearing in mind all the different circumstances and situations some people face in life, and the complexity that sometimes accompanies each circumstance, which makes it difficult for some to know which way to turn or proceed.

This book is written for anyone who feels alone and lost in this world—someone who thinks giving up is their only option and answer. Someone who feels uncertain, helpless, and forgets to love themselves or give themselves the care and love they truly deserve.

I understand how some situations in life can be so complicated and difficult for some to digest, let alone wrap your mind around. This then leaves you in a confused state of mind, and you wonder how you can wriggle yourself out from the chaos before you.

Moreover, I understand how things can be so sad and painful that it can make you feel alone and can make it difficult to trust or talk to anyone. You stay quiet instead, not just because you want to be quiet, but because you find it difficult to explain because it is so complicated in nature.

Well, I do feel you, and I have learned from experience that some matters in life require a delicate eye to help put things in perspective, and to open our hearts and help untangle the psychological war within us, inwardly and outwardly.

This book is a reminder that I understand and I get you. That I'm here with you.

This book touches many different aspects of life. With this book, I hope to invite wisdom, strength, self-understanding, clarity, self-help, reassurance, peace, hope, faith, love, happiness, and wellness into your life.

The idea of this book is to help you bring light to darkness and to help you love yourself, understand yourself, and treat yourself better.

Also to remind you that self-love is not an act of selfishness unless acted upon selfishly. Self-love and understanding is a vital thing in life, and it is important to our growth and well-being.

l say this because through the act of self-love and self-understanding, we can learn to love and understand others better too. The best of both worlds, I guess.

This book also highlights other psychological difficulties we are faced with in life, such as the lack of the will to live, lack of self-confidence, lack of self-esteem, self-doubt, the feeling of helplessness, and mental health issues.

I want to ease the battle within you, and help you make sense of uncertainty, so you can hopefully see through the darkness and sad times in your world. I want you to truly understand that you are not alone, no matter how confusing and complicated things are. My hope is that you will find the poems in this book useful to guide you through your experiences and whatever you are going through right now.

This book is not only about our personal difficulties. It also highlights matters relating to how we treat each other as human beings, while encouraging love, mindfulness, and a positive mindset.

I wrote this book for someone like you, because it is all about the things I feel you should know about yourself, your situation, your confusion, your feelings, your worries, your fears, your pain, and your hurt.

I hope that with this book you will find the strength and the wisdom to see things through, and that you will come out loving yourself and believing in yourself better than ever.

I hope that this book will remind you that you are important, special and unique in your own way, and that whatever the situation may be, your feelings count and matter, too. Through this book, you will find understanding, the healing and self-confidence to move forward, and the wisdom and power to take control of your own life. Moreover, you will find the strength, clarity, and sense to get up and out of any depressive state within you and shine like the beautiful and strong soul that you are.

The poems in this book are a reminder to you that you are not weak and that you are stronger than you think or know. I hope that this book will help you see through the challenges you are faced with and prepare you for all the good things that are coming to your life.

Most importantly, this book is also a reminder that you are worthy, loveable, beautiful, a wonderful person, and you deserve to be happy.

Finally, I hope that whatever you learn or gain from this book, you will use it to enhance the lives of others as you go along with your life.

May the peace of life be with you, my friend.

# Testament to You
## July 24, 2019

I can be a testament
to you.
And you can be testament
to another.

Together we can be a testament
to others—and the world.

# Recovery
## July 26, 2019

We are sometimes so happy
when it is all over.
But often neglect our recovery
time.
Always allow yourself time to
take it all in.

You need this, and it will help you
in moving forward, in your own way,
with clear thinking and peace of mind.

# Through Uncertainty to Certainty

*July 26, 2019*

> Sometimes, through uncertainty,
> we can find certainty
> and a new lease of life.

# Happenings and Reasons
## July 26, 2019

Anything that didn't happen,
didn't for a reason.
And everything that happened
did so for a reason too.

Be glad that you are getting
everything that is right
for you.

# Messenger
## July 26, 2019

I'm not interested in anything.
I'm just a learner and a messenger for you.

I want to be here for you.

And I love this role.

# Well-Placed

*July 30, 2019*

One day it will all fall into
place.
Keep your mind and heart
focused on the place
you want to be.
Soon, all will be well-placed for you
to see.

# Fine Art
## July 30, 2019

The act of fine imagination
often rewards you with the fine art
of life.
Using your imagination more can open doors
within you.

# The Good in You
## July 30, 2019

Some could be taking advantage of your good nature
and pretend to be helping you.
Sad, but don't let these negative acts
override the good in you.
There are people who truly deserve your
good nature.

# Trusted and Lost
## July 30, 2019

When you have trusted and lost so
much,
security often becomes
sketchy.
But we still need to live a life of
trust.
If you listen to your heart and intuition
before acting,
you will feel the sense of sketchiness
coming, if there is any.

Your heart knows the right ones to
trust, if you listen carefully.

It is nice to hear yourself.

Be attentive to you,
just like you would do when listening to
your teacher teaching your favorite
subject in class.

Give it all your attention,
and you will sense negativity
from a mile away.

# My Dreams and Yours
## July 30, 2019

One of my dreams is
to see your dreams
come true.
And to witness you
do well.

# Surroundings and Understandings

## July 30, 2019

We don't always need a great deal of
observation to understand
our surroundings.
But we often choose to see
what we want to see.

Which often limits our understanding
of our surroundings.

Nothing extreme; sometimes we just need to look openly
and pay attention to the ordinary details to see and understand
how things really are.

# Courage
*July 30, 2019*

Courage is an act of passion
and self-drive over what we
fear.
Having courage doesn't mean
we are fearless.
It just means we are
trying.

And you are doing great.

# Dreams and Depression
## July 30, 2019

Don't be depressed because you feel like
you have no dreams.
You do have dreams; they are just
hidden within you.

Get to know yourself,
and you will find your dreams.

We are all blessed with something.

But no one knows the limit of what they are
capable of as a human.
Even you have no idea how much you
are capable of.

Stay open to yourself.

You have a dream
and everything you need to lead
your own life.

# Togetherness

*August 10, 2019*

Togetherness without unity
is not togetherness.

Love bonds us and creates unity,
and unity holds us together.

The absence of love means
we are together in
emptiness.

And true unity can only exist
through love.

# The Lives of Others

*August 10, 2019*

The lives of others can be a lesson
to us all.
Only if we chose to
learn.

# Emotional Battery

*August 10, 2019*

We can be so caught up in all the
intensity and drama
that we sometimes forget the importance of
braking and recharging
our emotional
battery.
Remember, your lovely heart needs
a rest too.

# The Willing Ones
## August 11, 2019

They are willing to give their
lives.
They came when you
called.
They react to your
whisper.
Yet, they come home and scrape
by.
I feel you!
And I hope life will bring you fair treatment one day,
because you deserve better.

# Change of Heart

*August 11, 2019*

Sometimes a change of
heart is a sign of strength,
not weakness.

# Act of Love
## August 12, 2019

Being kind when no one is
watching is a pure act of
love.

# Runaway Feelings

*August 12, 2019*

Sometimes life can see us running away
from the ones we used to run to
for comfort.

# Rare Days

*August 23, 2019*

Some days are rare.

Embrace them with your
being.
Love them with your
heart.
Share them with your
soul.
Some days are rare.

# Misfit and Drift

*August 23, 2019*

In a world where everything looks the same,
and with just a handful of misfits,
no wonder we hardly know where
we belong.
No wonder we often appreciate those who
get our drift.
You are unique, and it is okay to
be different.
Different is a beautiful trend.

# Changes
## August 26, 2019

Sometimes you just need to
listen carefully to
feel the wind of
change.
Things are happening in your life
that you cannot always see immediately.

But be assured, there are changes happening
in your life.
And you will soon see for yourself.

# *What You Want*

## *August 26, 2019*

If you know what you want from love,
then love is worth
waiting for.

# Legacy
*September 6, 2021*

It is not always built on a family platform.
Your legacy can be built on the people around you.

# Your Highness
*September 25, 2019*

She carries herself
highly.
Her highness comes with
responsibilities.
She can deal with the
storms and sunshine.

An independent soul.

Her ways and style come
naturally.

That is why she is your
highness.

# Massive Load
## September 26, 2019

It is a massive load in itself to
pretend it is okay
when it isn't.

Be open about it.

Off load, and share it with
someone who cares.

Then you will feel the lightness within.

# Lights and Dreams

*September 29, 2019*

When you see the light of your
dreams,
don't let it quench.
For the light is the direction to that
dream destination of yours.

# The Perfectionist

*September 29, 2019*

Rather than always looking for
perfection,
accept your imperfection
and make life truly, perfectly splendid.

# The Zigzag Lane
*September 26, 2019*

Sometimes it may appear like the more
we hope for things to get better,
the worse they get.
Hold on, it will be okay in the end.
The road toward fulfilling our hope and dreams
is not always straight.

Sometimes it's a zigzag,
because there are things
you may need to learn along the way.

But you will get there.

It is better to get to your destination
with everything you need intact.
And the lessons of your journey can provide you
the things you need for
when you arrive.

# You Are Being Blessed
*October 15, 2019*

Your struggle, your experience, your pain, and hurt
is nothing to be ashamed of.
Be you and be proud of the road
you have come through.

You are being blessed.

You just don't know it yet.

# The Little Joy in My Heart

*October 16, 2019*

Giving with joy is a happiness only
true love can buy.

# Relax

*October 19, 2019*

It is difficult to find things
when you are worrying and beating
yourself up about them.

Relax and take a deep breath.

One day you will find
what you have been looking for in life.

# Nature's Time

*October 19, 2019*

Everyone has their time.
Don't worry, your time will come,
and it won't be long.

It is always best for things to happen
at their precise time.
With nature's time, you will hardly
miss anything.
But you will surely grow along the way
and attain your goals too.

# Sooner or Later

*October 20, 2019*

One day you will come to see why
everything happened the way it did.

Sooner or later, it will all make sense
and you will be pleased with the way things
have turned out.

# The Best of You
## *October 31, 2019*

You may not always know your best.

But doing your sincere best will walk you toward your very best.

Keep doing what you are doing.

# The Sleepless Nights and the Work Load

## April 6, 2020

From the surface, some things often look like they were easily achieved.
But below that surface, there is a great deal of hard work being applied
compared to how it is seen from the surface.
It is never really easy for anyone who is working hard to archive something
meaningful and great.
What you see on the surface is the result of
love,
time,
passion,
energy,
sacrifice,
courage,
and dedication.
Not to mention the pain and heartache
that accompany the journey and pursuit of
what you see on the surface.

Be proud of yourself, even when some refuse
to notice you.

# Spooks and Wheel
*September 3, 2020*

Sometimes when life
throws you spooks,

make a wheel of it,
and ride on.
The strength you need
is within you.

I'm sure you already know that life is not always
a comfortable bed of roses.

But you also have the built-in ability to cope
and adapt to circumstances,
and the wisdom to
see it through.

Sometimes we can take difficult circumstances
and turn them into positive situations.

# Your Precious Time

*September 3, 2020*

You could be emotionally intelligent and smart.
But in some circumstances,
life may just require you to be strong,
not to fight it, but to move on
in good grace.
Some things are not worth the hassle you feel inside,
and your time is precious.

# Deliberate Act

*September 3, 2020*

It is far better to let it go
than to give into the deliberate acts of others.

They are just people who wants nothing
good for you.

No need to bother.

# Answers to Your Questions

*September 3, 2020*

Sometimes what you don't understand or know now,
just means you are not there yet.

Trust that, in time,
you will understand all that your heart seeks to know.

Relax, be patient,
and answers will find their way to you,
and the know-how will follow suit.

# Uncertainty

*September 3, 2020*

To make sense of certain things in life
is not always easy.
But I pray and hope that one day
life will help you make sense of the
dark clouds that surround you
and bring you a ray of visibility with a dash of
starlight to make sense of
your dark times.

# Wind of Change
## September 3, 2020

Just because you are not seeing physical change
doesn't mean that change isn't
happening.
Sometimes, it depends on which spectacles
you are looking from.

Change is all around us.

You will see, if you look and listen carefully.
Or simply give it some time
and look back later,
and you will see that you are not where you thought
you were anymore.

You are growing and moving forward.

# Capturing Moments in Motion
*September 4, 2020*

Sometimes, in the end,
it is one moment that changes everything
for the better.
It is also one moment that sparks
wonderful things.
I pray that when that moment comes,
you will have all it takes to capture the moment,
because it is one moment that brings a turning point
in one's life.

# Someone like You
## September 4, 2020

This day reminds me of the natural beauty and magic
the universe holds when we are open and willing to share it
with someone who cares.

Someone like you.

# The Ordinary Love
*September 5, 2020*

When both lives are free in a relationship,
and the foundation is based on
common trust,
your life and relationship can be so
amazing.

And love can be so ordinary,
but unique underneath.

# My Appreciation for You
*September 5, 2020*

Today I thought of you,
and I just want to let you know that I notice you
and everything you do.

And I really do appreciate
your lovely heart.

# Weakest Moment
*September 5, 2020*

Sometimes when you are at your weakest,
and you have nowhere else to turn,
surrender yourself to life.

Take a step back.

Look within and ask life to bring you the
strength to cope.

Trust, and you will feel
the strength.

# Outskirts

*September 5, 2020*

Sometimes people will misjudge you.
Don't worry, be you.
In the end, your true outskirts
will shine through for them to see.

# Strange Characters
*September 6, 2020*

Some will say you can't do it.
Then you do it.
And they will hate
you for it.

Don't worry about these kinds.

Be with the kind that support your growth.

You owe positive influence to yourself,
because you can choose which influences you
invite into your life,
or to surround yourself with.

# Sense of Distance
## September 6, 2020

Sometimes when things are already difficult for you.
Some will act like they care,
but they will be secretly and deliberately
trying to make things even more difficult for you,
knowing the weight of your current load.

I hope, if you sense these kinds of people in your life,
you will have the sense
to distance yourself too.

# Act of Care
## September 6, 2020

Sometimes it is the very people that
we didn't expect to care
that surprise us.

# Consequent of No

*September 10, 2020*

They will always say you are very nice
until you say "no".
Then they will start saying you are
horrible.

Never mind.

# The Best
*September 10, 2020*

You are the best of all.

That is why all the best are
within your reach.

# The Difference Is Clear

*September 10, 2020*

The right ones with shoulders to cry on
can make all the difference.
Know who you are confiding in,
for the wrong ones will bring nothing
but miseries that you don't need.

# New Life
## September 18, 2020

Anyone can fall into a state of depression.
It is how you end it or get out
that matters.
Suicide is not the way.
At least, let's talk about it first,
just in case there is a new life around the corner here
on earth for you that you can't yet see.

# Surprises
*September 20, 2020*

If the ones you believe in keep letting you down,
try the ones you didn't believe in.

They may surprise you.

# Got the Gist
*September 21, 2020*

You gave them a hint,
and you were hoping they would ask,
"What's the matter?"

They didn't, so you kept
everything quiet.

It is okay to want to stay quiet.

But it is better to open up at the right time,
with the right people.

# With You in It

*September 28, 2020*

It is a wonderful world with you in it.

And the ones who know you best,
know it too.

# Without You
## September 28, 2020

A world without you isn't
wonderful at all,
because you radiate
happiness.

And happiness is what you bring to others.

# Positive Energy
## November 20, 2020

It is better to give love, even to the ones
who mistreat you.
But be wise and wary of the energy
you let in.

# Unnecessary Analysis

*November 20, 2020*

Sometimes you don't need to be analytical,
when it is all clear to you.
You just need to trust your instincts
and do what you know
is right for you.

# The Opportunity for Growth
## November 20, 2020

What you gather and learn
from each situation,
it is your opportunity for
growth,
and you should take advantage of each lesson.

# Positive Detachment
## November 20, 2020

We all need strength to grow,
and the moment you start realizing the things
that drain you emotionally and mentally
and start walking away from them,
the sooner you will be toxic energy free.
Sometimes, we need to be detached in order to
breathe and see clearly.

# I'm So Happy for You
## November 20, 2020

Even though you may not want
much from life,
you deserve the peace of mind and happiness
that is coming to you.

I'm so happy for you.

# Jealous Minds

*November 22, 2020*

Sometimes, with every fall,
there is a climb.
Some are there to catch
you when you fall.
Some are simply wishing
for your fall.
But it is not always about
ups and downs.
Sometimes you just have to watch the level ground
you stand and walk on so you don't get
tripped by tricky minds.

# The Best of Tomorrow
## November 22, 2020

I hope your today will be better than
your yesterday.
And your tomorrow will be even better
than your today.

# Sense of Humor
## *November 22, 2020*

If you are clever, it is nice.
If you are intellectual, it is nice too.
But it is also amazing to have a sense of
humor.

# How We Talk

*November 22, 2020*

It is one thing to talk with
people.
And it is another thing to talk at
people
while thinking you are talking
with them.

# From Their Eyes
December 2, 2020

After they upset you,
if you say nothing, they will think
you are boiling.
When your mind wanders off, they will wonder how
you are going to react.

If you stay too quiet, they will think you
have hidden plans.

But the truth is,
sometimes you are just in your own world,
wondering along and dealing with things.

What is in your heart is completely different from
the assumptions they hold.
Even in your darkest of times, I hope you
will keep your light on
so they can see through their own dark acts,
and realize they are manipulating
no one, but themselves.

Life is with you.

# The Chance
## December 10, 2020

Sometimes the best thing to do for someone
is to give them a chance.

Let them be, grow, and shine
in their own ways.

# Dark Times
*October 12, 2020*

Don't worry, even in our
darkest times,
we are never really alone.

A light is hidden within that
darkness.

Soon you will find it.

And when you do, please pinpoint your light,
just like you do when using
Google geocode to
pinpoint a location.

Pinpoint your light and follow the line of your light
for directions.
Soon you will be walking along destiny lane,
heading toward your own destiny.

Life is behind you my friend.

.

# The Knock

When insight comes knocking at your conscious mind,
open the door.

It takes an intuition to
get an insight,
and wisdom to work through it.

And sometimes we have to be diplomatic when it
comes to how we navigate the route of our insight
in order to get a profound result.

# I Hope
*December 22, 2020*

I hope that, when the time comes,
you will remember that however
things might seem,
that does not always reflect the truth of
how they are.

# Done and Dusted

*December 11, 2020*

When it is all done and dusted,
just remember what you have
learned.

# Try a Little Harder
## December 13, 2020

Sometimes it takes more than
just doing enough to achieve
something great.

Keep working on it until you reach the
desired destination.

You are nearly there anyway.

# *Dear You*
## *December 29, 2020*

A life with purpose is a life worth living
and striving toward,
my dear friend.
Living a life that means something to you
means you are on a journey toward
internal happiness.

# Own Your Strength
*September 30, 2020*

The weak see fear and act quickly to please.
You are not weak, dear.
You are a thing of
strength.

So own it.

# You Are Home

*September 30, 2020*

Wherever you are
will always be home to so many,
because homely is how you make people feel
when they are with you.

# Confusing Eh!
### September 1, 2020

They will say, "Oh I'm different, I'm not like her or him."
Then later, they will start acting different.

It is confusing, but that doesn't mean that
they don't love you.
Sometimes people go through their own
ups and downs within.

But if you can take yourself out of the
confusing feelings and the conflicting appearances
before you and look again,
you will see the truth as it is.

Sometimes people react to the
ups and downs going on within them outwardly.

And they often portray conflicting impressions
without realizing it.

Hopefully, all is well.

# Mind You

*September 1, 2020*

When you act and respond according to
their behavior
they will say you are two-faced.
Surely, they can't be spiteful
and expect you to smile
like all is well,
even though you can see through their
colored behavior and act.

# Sense of Understanding
*September 1, 2020*

Your sense of understanding can set you apart from some, and can also draw you closer to the right people.

# You Are Dynamic
*September 8, 2020*

Being dynamic in life, isn't two-faced.
It just means you can relate to different
things and people.

# It Depends on You
*October 31, 2020*

Everything depends on how much
you are open to it.
The more open you are within,
the more you will learn,
and the clearer things will become.

# Life Won't Pass You By
*October 31, 2020*

In life, everything has its moment.

Live your life by the natural timing of life,
and embrace these moments
as you go along.

Sometimes the road can be smooth,
and sometimes it can be rough.

But be assured,
life won't pass you by.

# Let Them Know
*October 31, 2020*

I do know that I'm not perfect.

And I do make mistakes, too,
just like every other human.

But I will never knowingly do you wrong.

# Understanding Love
## November 1, 2020

We can't fully love
until we fully understand love.

Love is freedom and wellness.
Love is a place where you surrender all
and still feel safe.
Love is a place of no fear.
Love only contains love.
Love is quietly beautiful.
Love has no worries.
Love harbors no negativity.
Love is compassionate and understanding.
Love is the peace and beauty we feel inside.
Love is what feels natural and in sync.
Love is the only thing that will ever truly bring
us the comfort we need in life.

# Your Kindness Is Beautiful
*November 1, 2020*

Ah, I understand that the world
can be so cold that it could turn a kind soul
into a ball of ice.
But don't let this coldness stop you
from giving to those souls
who truly deserve your
kindness.

# Good Men
*December 22, 2020*

There isn't a perfect man,
but there are many
good men.

# Not Your Cup of Tea
*December 22, 2020*

Not getting involved
doesn't mean you don't like them.

You like them.

But some things are just not
your cup of tea.

# The Perfect One You Wished For
*December 22, 2020*

Don't sit there waiting and looking for the
perfect one
when the perfect one has been right in front
of you all along.

# You Are Not an Alliance

*December 22, 2020*

Just because they confided in you
doesn't mean you are now
their ally.

You listened and sympathized
with them.
But you wished both parties
the best, because your heart only wants the
best for everyone.

Your fairness is something
of beauty.

And you have a beautiful mind,
dear.

# Our World

*December 25, 2020*

Time will come.

We will end the war between
our worlds.

We will be too cool for war.

And together we will act as one force to
protect our world.

All you have to do, is do
your bit.

And your bit will surely make a change
that you can't always see
immediately.

But the changes are there and naturally impacting the
world.

# Behind the Shadows of Others
*December 28, 2020*

Don't hide behind their shadows.
Your light is brighter than you think or know.

# Love and Cherish Her

*December 29, 2020*

If you love and cherish her,
she will always take care of
you.
You will feel a kind of wellness beyond
your imagination.

One like you have never
felt before.

# Not Okay
## January 1, 2021

It is not okay if they keep
letting you down when you need them the most.

# *You*

*January 2, 2021*

The world is dark without you.

Without you there is no moonlight to help us see through the dark.

# You Are

*January 2, 2021*

You are everything beautiful,
and everything beautiful reminds the world of you.

# Too Emotional

*January 3, 2021*

They will say you are too emotional
until they need your emotional understanding.
It is okay to be emotional,
but be strong when you need to.

# The Happier the Better

*January 3, 2021*

The less you expect from others,
the more content you will feel,
and the happier you will be.

# The Fight to Survive

*January 4, 2021*

Don't fight it.
Maybe this is how it is supposed to be
before it gets better.
Life has its own way of arranging things for us.
It might not always be a straight road,
but all will become clear in time.

Sometimes a zigzag road can lead you to your
destination too.
The roughness of our journey in life
often provides us with the relevant experiences
we need to live our lives.

# Good and Bad

*January 4, 2021*

Everyone wants to be your friend
when things are good.
But only one in a few will be your friend
when things are bad.

# Seen Enough
*January 7, 2021*

You might not have seen it all.

But you have seen enough
to learn a lot.

# Mindfulness
## *January 8, 2021*

Sometimes what goes on outside of a person's head
is completely different from what is
going on inside.

They may not be as stable as you think.

# You Are a Ray of Sunshine

*January 23, 2021*

The weather man said it will be
stormy and raining
today.
Then you came along, like a ray of sunshine
piercing through the storm and lighting
up the sky with your
sunny outlook.

# This Is So You
## January 26, 2021

Only your presence can turn tonic
into fresh water.
While your absence makes
face water run.

You are something special.

# Hurting Us versus Loving You
*January 26, 2021*

I love you so much that hurting you means
hurting myself.
And loving myself means loving you
even better.

To love yourself, is to love others.

# Beautiful Things

*January 26, 2021*

Days like these make me happy,
because I'm writing the beautiful things
I want to share with you.

# My Wish

## January 26, 2021

The duty of life is not a work of
honor.
It is a privilege to perform the
work of life.
And my wish is to serve you.

# Flaws

*January 26, 2021*

Yesterday you said I was your
ray of sunshine.
Today you are acting like I'm your
thunderstorm.

Either way, I'm with you.
Together we will brave the weather,
because I love your flaws and imperfections.

# You Will Survive

*January 26, 2021*

I watched you watching me
struggle.
I saw the smile on your
face too.
I hope that I will survive and, one day,
I hope you will smile the same way
you are smiling now.

I pray that the faces that laughed at your struggles,
will one day laugh at your success too.

# What Matters

*January 26, 2021*

Some may misjudge you
and describe you how they want.
But it doesn't really matter.

You know who you are, and that is what matters.

# The Right Ones

*January 29, 2021*

Sometimes things may not work out right
for many different reasons.
But be grateful for all the right things unfolding
in your life.

They are the right ones for you.

# You Will Get There

*January 29, 2021*

Sometimes it can take a little while.
But you will get there,
and you will see.
Be gentle with yourself.

# Perfect Life
## January 29, 2021

A perfect life is the one where you are truly happy and content.

# Our Needs

## *January 30, 2021*

Sometimes our needs may not be
useful to our real purpose in life.

# You Are Strong

*January 31, 2021*

Sometimes, you just need to look in the mirror
and remind yourself that you are the
strongest person you know,
because you are.

# Your Ways
*January 31, 2021*

Despite the ice balls thrown at you,
they made you stronger, and warmer,
not ice cold.

You are wonderful.

# Say So

*January 31, 2021*

It is sad to live in a pretend world.

Acting like it is okay
when it isn't.

If it isn't, just say so.

# Only You
## *February 1, 2021*

Only you know where it
hurts.

Only you know how and what you feel
inside,
and only you can take care of yourself
like no one else
can.

Only you know what is right for
you.

So act accordingly.

# Go Easy
*February 3, 2021*

Go easy on yourself.
Whatever got you here, will take you there.
Life is not just about the destination,
it is about the journey itself too.

Take all the roughness in stride,
and enjoy the ride.

You will be okay.

# Moving On
## February 3, 2021

Let them do what they want to do.

Let them say what they want to say.

You do what you have to do
anyway.

Sometimes, the best decision is to say nothing.
Let go and move on.

# Hello

## February 4, 2021

I just want you to know that
you are amazing.
I feel what you are
going through.

Something tells me you are going to do right,
and that everything will turn out
well for you.
Life has something good
in store for you too.
And these gloomy days will
soon pass.

Stay strong, it is nearly over.

# Together minus Togetherness
## February 4, 2021

It is better to live apart
than to live together without
togetherness.

# Be Truthful about It
## February 7, 2021

Some will say they don't care,
while deep down it is
eating them up.
Don't pretend with your
feelings.

# My Dear
## February 7, 2021

I just want you to know that,
no matter how long it takes,
it will come.

It is written in your destiny.

It is destined to happen,
and you will see.

Your struggle will bless you with
value.
Your pain will reward you with
strength.

# Misjudgment
## February 12, 2021

It is better to be careful when passing
judgment on others,
because we sometimes don't know
what they are thinking and why they do
things the way they do.
Sometimes people do things for
reasons completely different from our own.

# That Person

*February 12, 2021*

Always appreciate that special
person you know.

That special person that is in
your world.

They deserve to be known and
celebrated.

# Be Picky
## February 12, 2021

Just because you didn't say something
doesn't mean you are
foolish.
Some things are just not worth
responding to.

Be picky with what you
respond to.

# The Finest Study
## February 14, 2021

The finest study you could ever partake in is the study of yourself and what life means to you.

# Well
## February 14, 2021

I hope the ones around you
will hang around when you cry.

I hope they will stay when the sky before you
feels like a total eclipse
in daylight.

# Delicate Eyes

*February 15, 2021*

Sometimes, when matters become hard to
untangle,
it takes a delicate and careful eye to
untangle them.

Let yourself be.

Look carefully within, be true to yourself.
Then you will see the way forward
for yourself.

# Inside Out
## February 18, 2021

Life isn't about how beautiful you are on the
outside.
It is about how beautiful you are on the
inside.
So let your inner beauty shine
out.

# Talented

*February 24, 2021*

I think you are much better
than you think you are.

You should be doing something with your
knowledge and gift.

It is amazing, how talented you are,
but you don't even know it.

# Loving You
## February 24, 2021

Most of all, you deserve someone who will be in
love with you.
Not someone who takes your love
for granted.

# Failure and Success

## February 24, 2021

It is nice to be happy about what
you gained from failure.

Sometimes these things propel you
to success, and to what is
meant to be.

Never regret trying.

# It Is Better

## February 24, 2021

It is better to take what life offers you
than to fight it.
Appreciate it, learn to work with it,
and let the rest unfold.

# The Diggers
## February 26, 2021

They will dig and dig
until you say something,
then they will say you are the
bad guy.

If you spot them heading toward you with a shovel,
keep your distance.

You don't need the ones who dig at you.

Be with the ones who dig your style.

# Words between the Lines
## February 26, 2021

We hear words with our ears.
But our intuition can hear words
in between the lines of what is
said and unsaid.

# Trust Yourself
## February 26, 2021

Sometimes, things may sound right
but feel wrong.
Trust yourself, and let your intuition be
your guide.

# Kind Heart
*March 2, 2021*

I went to sleep thinking I had done
something good.
Only to wake up in a
battlefield.
I hope your kindness will never bring you
heartache.

# The Missing Puzzle Piece
*March 5, 2021*

I hope that, one day, you will find the
answers and relief you seek.

I pray that life will bring you the
missing puzzle piece you seek.

And I trust that one day, all will unfold
before your eyes.
Tears will drop, and you will look up to the sky
with gratitude.

# Your Intentions

## March 5, 2021

Your intentions are good,
and that counts.

# Something I Hope
# You Don't Forget

*March 5, 2021*

Sometimes it is the little things we do
that makes another person feel
like somebody.

I hope you don't forget this.

# Willing to Give
*March 6, 2021*

Some don't really want anything apart from
hoping that you will appreciate them for who they are.

But they are willing to give.

# The Good Things
### March 7, 2021

I will always remember all the good things
you did for me.

Never forget the heart that
did good for you.

# Curious Mind
*March 7, 2021*

Don't run away from knowledge,
embrace it instead.

Allow yourself to be curious,
and let your mind wonder.

# Right Direction
*March 8, 2021*

Everything in life is step-by-step.

You may be slow, but at least
you are learning and moving in the
right direction.

# We Are All Strange
*March 8, 2021*

It is okay to think something is
strange.
But it is unwise to mock something
you have no knowledge about.

The deeper you dive into
yourself and your mind,
the sooner you will realize that
we are all strange
after all.

# Lift Up
## March 8, 2021

One day you will be fine.
Life will lift you up.
Nothing remains the same
forever.
Your shining soul is not meant
to be stuck in a rut.

# The Game

## March 9, 2021

I know the game.

And I understand the game.

But I'm not playing the game.
When it comes to life,
I don't play games.

Your life and emotions are not a
board game for anyone.
Leave those who want to play,
to it.
But remove yourself from
the picture.

# Your Feelings Matter Too
## March 9, 2021

Be loyal to your feelings,
and don't allow your feelings
to be someone else's Nintendo GameCube
or playground.

# Cynic Free
## March 9, 2021

Even if you don't like them,
you don't need to be hateful or
spiteful.
Keep your heart cynic free
and open for finer
things.

# Overcoming Troubles
*March 11, 2021*

Nothing will ever be the same again,
after that day.
But I hope you will find peace and happiness
within yourself.

# The Best in You

*March 13, 2021*

Keep it cool and don't worry,
their negativity will only
bring out the
best in you.

# Relativity
## March 13, 2021

We want to understand but refuse to
relate.
We want to learn but refuse to be
open.
It is tough to understand things
if we can't truly relate and keep an
open mind.

# Openness
## March 14, 2021

Focus on what you know,
but be open to the things
you don't
know.

# The Takers

Even when you have little
and still give generously.

They will think you have a lot
and keep digging until
there is a hole in your
pocket.

And when there is nothing left,
you become nothing too, just like your
empty pocket.

# It is Getting Better
## March 16, 2021

Even if today is not as good as you
would have like it to be,

you are better than where
you were yesterday.

This is progress, and a good thing too.

# Relative
## March 17, 2021

I hope that, one day, others will come to realize that
we are all relative after all.

# Spotting the Difference
## March 18, 2021

Some are there to improve your
well-being.
Others are there to hinder your
growth.
Spot the difference and act
accordingly.

You are not being selfish.

You are just doing what is right for you.

# Healing Is Revealing
## March 18, 2021

The more you heal,
the more revealing it becomes.
And the more your point of view
becomes clear.

# The Closest Ones
## March 19, 2021

Sometimes it is the ones closest to you
that you need to watch out for.
They are often the ones that can
manipulate and hurt you without
you seeing it coming.

# Your Mate

*March 19, 2021*

You know that person you can talk to
and be silly with?
That one that doesn't judge you
but always has your back?

That is your mate.

# These Days
## March 19, 2021

Even just waking up every morning
is a blessing for me
these days.
I hope you will find life beautiful enough
to be glad you are awake
each morning.

# Own Your Life
## March 19, 2021

One of the biggest mistakes you
could ever let yourself make is
to allow another person
to tell you how to
think and act.

# Two Souls

*March 19, 2021*

And they picked up where they left off.

# Merging Souls
## March 19, 2021

And just like that, two souls are clicked.

# Joyous People
*March 19, 2021*

Even when I have no joy in my life,
the joy in you gives me joy.
So one way or the other,
I'm still getting some joy,
because I'm happy to see you joyous.

# The Lost Voices
## March 19, 2021

I hope that someone will be there for you,
and speak for you, if you ever
lose your voice.

# Stress Free
## March 19, 2021

It is surprising how much stress can cost you,
and it is amazing how much a
stress-free mind can bring to your life.

Peace is needed to function.

# Silent Objectives
*March 20, 2021*

I see the negatives too,
but I don't talk about them much
because I look for ways to bring the positives
out of the negatives, and share them
with you.

# My Beautiful Friend
## March 20, 2021

You remind me of something out of a movie.
Only you can represent Kim K. in a beauty contest,
and walk on a runway like Beyoncé.

Your beauty, inside and out, is a cause for
celebration.

Don't let a lack of self-esteem get
the better of the super you.

# The Love You Give
## March 24, 2021

Most of all, you deserve someone that
will be in love with you.

Being in love with someone who's not in love with you
is a sad way to live life.
And it is lovely in itself to be in love with someone
who's in love with you.

Your happiness lies here, and you
deserve this.

# Silent Words

*March 26, 2021*

I listened to everything
you didn't say.
And I felt everything
you wanted.
I'm here with you.

# *You Are Your First Love*
## *March 26, 2021*

You know how to love
because you loved yourself
first.

# This Time
*March 26, 2021*

You can start all over again, knowing you were wrong
the first time, and this time
you are going to
do well.

Never give up on you!

# The Good Fellow and the Outsider

March 26, 2021
(Dedicated to MC Bravado)

I know how I felt when I was alone and
cast out.
I also know how I felt when a good fellow came
to my aid.

Now, all I want to do is share my lessons with you
and enrich you with the wisdom and love
from the good fellow.

# The Original You
## March 28, 2021

Be honest about how you feel.
Say it as you really feel.

The heart you are talking to will capture
your true originality.

# Being Open
## March 31, 2021

Openness is the key to understanding.

When you open your heart and mind
to something.

Suddenly everything becomes clearer.

# Growth Killer

*March 31, 2021*

The biggest killer of growth is stress.
It can throw your concentration off too.

# The Uncomplicated Version
## March 31, 2021

Life can sometimes be straightforward,
unless you want the complicated version.
Seek for the vertical version,
where everything is
straightforward.

Life is not as complicated as we think.
Sometimes we make it complicated
for ourselves.
Knowing who you are, what you want,
and what you are doing is the key to unlocking the
entrance to your route, and the starting point to
living the life you want.

# Some People
## March 31, 2021

The more you learn about some people,
the less you feel inclined to judge.

People often have different reasons for their
thoughts and behavior.

# Right but Uncomfortable
## March 5, 2021

It is okay if doing what is right makes you
feel uncomfortable for a little while.

Trust that this feeling will pass for brighter ones.
Hang in there!

You are on the road to right things
and a right mind.

# Unfounded Imagination
## March 5, 2021

Sometimes it is the very people who do you wrong that
create their own worries by picking through your
every written word to find a relative meaning to
their thoughts and fears.

They may even start preparing for a battle
that only exists in their
imagination.

# The Run Away Year
## March 5, 2021

Maybe everything that happened,
happened for us to understand
something about life and
our world.
Even though we are all relatives,
we never really relate to one another like
relatives.
Maybe that's why 2020 was a year of sadness, loss, and grief,
so we can learn to love, appreciate,
and give.
Through love, we will find peace.
Through peace we will find
understanding.
When we are at peace,
the world will be at
peace.

Maybe 2020 was just a year to learn.

The year we all went back to the school
of thoughts and relativity.
The year we had no choice but to allow
life to educate us.

It may feel like a runaway year,
but take a look within yourself again,
and you will realize how much you have
learned and gained.

A lot has changed,
and you are not the same person
you were back then.

That is a good thing.

# Even When They Are Wrong

*March 31, 2021*

Even if they are wrong,
allow them the time to understand
how and why they are wrong.

Only then can they truly learn
something.

# Jealousy Is a Disease

*March 20, 2021*

It eats you up from the
inside.
It puts you in a bitter state with
yourself.
Supporting the good and growth of
others will bring you a healthy
mind and life.

# Twenty-four Seven Calls
## March 20, 2021

Watch how those twenty-four seven calls drop
to zero when they don't need you
anymore.

Don't allow yourself to be used by
anyone.

You are better than that.

Learn to do things for those who really
deserve your doings.
Appreciate the ones who appreciate
you.
My dear, please, lose the ones who only
wish to use you.

# You Are Not a Mug

*March 21, 2021*

Some will want you to do things for them.
Things they would never dream about doing for you,
let alone actually doing it.

Be wise with your kindness.
Don't allow others to take your
kindness for foolishness.

# The Vibes They Give
## March 20, 2021

My friend, the funny thing about vibes is that
it doesn't matter how close or far away
you are from others,

you will always feel their vibes if you are
aware and pay attention.

Vibes don't lie, they are revealing.

So act accordingly,
my friend.

# Dear Friend
## March 20, 2021

A little while ago, I was your friend.
I woke up one day to find out we were not
friends anymore.

What changed?

Did I do you wrong?

Did I purge you unknowingly?

Not sure, but all I can remember, as I sift through
my thoughts, is that I came whenever
you called.

But it is okay, some are not here to stay
when things are broken.
They will leave in no time when
things fall apart.

# Lessons of Struggle

*March 20, 2021*

The lessons of your struggle can change
everything and bring you all the things
money cannot buy.

# School of Life
## March 20, 2021

They are your teacher, and it is because of them
you are doing well at the
school of life.

You are turning their negative acts into
positive lectures for yourself.

# Shocking
*March 20, 2021*

You know what baffles me?
How someone can take and take from you
but watch you struggle
with a smile on
their face.

# You and Them

*Marc 20, 2021*

You can carry them when they need your
help and support,
but you can't carry their jealousy and hatred
toward others or yourself too.

# In Your World

## March 20, 2021

The only mistake you made was inviting someone who has no care for you into your world.

But, at least, you learned something.

# Positive Envy
## March 20, 2021

How does one get jealous?
Honestly, I don't know,
because I'm too busy being happy
and wanting what's best for you.
If I envy you at all, it is because you inspire me,
you leave me with the splendid thoughts and
the positive drive to be like you
in my own way.

# Faults of Our Own Making

*March 20, 2021*

I know how you feel.

You guess it is your fault.

Your heart told you to stay away from them,
but your sympathetic nature
won't let you.

Don't beat yourself up about it.

You are just a nice person, and that is a
beautiful trait to have.

But we do live and learn too.

# The Good Things
## March 20, 2021

Sometimes, when things were so bad,
it takes a long time to get used to them
being good.
Let's hope it doesn't take you as long
as it took you to get here,
to get used to it,
because you deserve every moment of the good things
that are unfolding in your life.

# Something You Should Know
*March 20, 2021*

I just want you to know that
there are people in this world
who don't know you
in person,
but care about you because the gift of caring
is in their nature.
And they can feel what you are going through right now,
and they wish for that pain and sadness to
leave you alone.

I'm one of them, and
I'm here with
you.

# The Sweet Smell of Love
## March 20, 2021

The most pungent smell in the world
is hatred.
And the most pleasant smell in the
world is love.

Take a few seconds to feel it,
and you will smell the
difference.

# Saying Something
## March 21, 2021

Sometimes, not saying anything
is saying something.

# Tighten Your Belt
## March 21, 2021

Tighten your belt for now,
and be ready to wade the storm.

I'll definitely see you on the other side, because
I know you will see this through.

# The Sweet Thing

*March 21, 2021*

The sweet thing about you is that,
even if you have reasons
not to like someone,

you still want the best for them
anyway.

And I think this is inspiring.

# The Lost Souls of the World

*March 21, 2021*

I don't know if ghosts are real or not,
but from what I have seen in
movies,
a lost soul in this world is like a ghost
walking around with no place
to call home.

No people to call their people.

Even when standing among millions,
they remain unnoticed, just like
the ghost in the
movies.

People may ghost you,
but life won't ghost you.

Something is watching over you.

# Self-Clarity
*March 24, 2021*

By being open with yourself,
you will able to see
yourself more clearly and be open to
others.

# Emotional

*March 24, 2021*

True, you are very emotional.

But you are very
strong too.

That's why you can't be
anyone's ride.

# Tiring Love
## March 24, 2021

It is quite tiring to love people
who don't love you.

True, I understand, but love them
anyway.

You can love people and not be with
the people.

Love is about what you feel
in your heart.

And it is a nice quality, to practice the
act of love.

The ones that will love you will find
their way into your life.

The love you give will come to you
abundantly.

But what you get in return, is not the
reason to love.

It is just beautiful to love and be loved.

# The Dreams They Chase
March 24, 2021

If a person's dream is to drag
another person down,

then that may just explain why
they are not progressing in their
personal life.

# Your Role
## March 24, 2021

You said sorry for the role you
played.
But you're not responsible for the role others
played.

They are.

# Authentic Feelings
March 24, 2021

When it comes to it,
share your authentic feelings.

Otherwise, anything else
is a waste of your precious time and breath.

# Parts of Maturity
## March 25, 2021

Maturity is when you become selective of what you do
and how you do it,
what you respond to and how you
respond to it.

# Just Tired
## March 25, 2021

You are not upset with them.
You are just quiet and distant,
because you are tired of being around people
who don't care
but act like they care.

So you are just tired.

And that is understandable.

# PlayStation
## March 25, 2021

The other day, I played FIFA 2005 on my
slimline PlayStation,
Chelsea versus Spurs.
But all I could think about was you.
Even though things didn't turn out well for us,
I still miss you, my friend.

I guess some friends will always
remain special, regardless.

# The Ones That Matters

## March 26, 2021

If the ones that matter are
happy for you, then that is
what matters.

# Now

*March 26, 2021*

Sometimes we waste our time and moments
being preoccupied with what the
future holds, while missing
out on now.

# It Is Okay To Ask
*March 30, 2021*

It is better to ask when you are
unsure than to assume you know
when you really
don't know.

# Okay with It
## March 31, 2021

They meant everything to you.

But it was sad to see that you
meant nothing to them.

And you have learned to be
okay with it.

Your strength is admirable.

# Mind Games
## April 2, 2021

If you keep punishing and manipulating the heart
that loves you,
one day they will walk away from you for good.

Be sincere with the heart that
loves you.

# The Price for Winning
## April 2. 2021

Sometimes, in life,
it is better to lose some battles
than win them.
For some winnings sometimes come with
their own battle and price to pay.

# Honest Feelings

*April 2, 2021*

It is not that you don't care,
you do.
But you only have time for
honest feelings.

And you are right to
feel this way.

# Our Nemesis
## April 4, 2021

Sometimes, our biggest nemesis is our
inability to be decisive.
Therefore, we act and speak and try
to play fair, all the while
leaving others with the logical
advantage and decisiveness
over us and matters.

# That Night and the Weeks That Followed

*April 5, 2021*

Only you and your creator know how much
you cried that night, and how little you
slept in the weeks
that followed.

We are just happy to see you
where you are now.

Amazing!

# The Human Ways
## April 8, 2021

Sometimes, we pass through certain people for
reasons unknown to us.

And every passage brings or takes away
something from our lives without us
even knowing.

You can feel the shift, if attuned.

Some take our worries and fears away
while bringing us strength and clarity
for development.

Some take our troubles away and make
room for better things.

Sometimes, even the smallest human exchange
can create a shift and change within
another person.

Be nice, be mindful, you don't know who
you may be helping or who may be
helping you.

# Dark Days
## April 9, 2021

Even when my days are dark,
I still have hope and faith
to see the light one day.

Stay strong, and you will see the brighter
side of life soon.

# Bad Night
*April 10, 2021*

I hope your tonight will be better
than last night.
I hope you will sleep well without
any worries on your mind
to keep you awake.

# Real Love
*April 11, 2021*

I hope one day you will find someone
to love you as much you love him or her,
because you deserve
only real love.

# Their Route
## April 11, 2021

Don't judge them until you have travelled
through their route.

# It Is Okay to Try and Fail
## April 12, 2021

It is better to try and fail
than to sit there not trying
and later wondering what
could have been.
At least, by trying, you will have answers
and you will learn too,
even if you fail.

# Sense and Expectation

*April 13, 2021*

It makes no sense to expect someone
without sense to show
sensibility.

# The Reflection in the Mirror
April 13, 2021

It is okay to give some care and love to
that person you see in the mirror
right in front of you.

# Sharing It
*April 13, 2021*

It hasn't been easy,
but nobody knows.

I hope you will find the strength to
share it when the time is
right for you.

# Praying for You
*April 13, 2021*

I was thinking about what I should
ask for from God.
Then I remembered that I asked for a few
things yesterday.
So, I use today's request on
you instead.
I asked God to bring you all the things
you need.

Most importantly, happiness.

# Loved Ones

## April 14, 2021

The people who love you will always
want to see you do well.

# Ah!
*April 14, 2021*

You really are a breath of fresh air to
those around you.

# You Deserve Better

*April 15, 2021*

You are not better than them or anyone
in this world.
But you are better than the way
you are treated.

# Room to Learn

*April 17, 2021*

Give them time to learn, some people don't really
know what they are doing at the beginning.

# Unusual Feelings

*April 17, 2021*

Kindness usually makes people
happy.
Mind you, some have to get used to it,
because it is the unusual for them.

# Talk and Joke

## April 17, 2021

It is a beautiful thing to be with someone you can just talk to and joke with.

# Beautiful Star
## April 19, 2021

I think you are very pretty with the
makeup on.
But I saw a beautiful star before
the makeup.

Either way, you are beautiful and mesmerizing
to see.

# I Get You
## April 19, 2021

I know what it is like to be unappreciated,
and I understand how it feels to be
looked down upon.

I also get how it feels to not be loved
by the very ones who
are supposed to
love you.

# Creating Your Happiness
*April 19, 2021*

> I think the greatest achievement in life
> is to see other humans benefit
> from something they have
> created.

# The Painted Society

April 19, 2021

Sometimes we wear our fine attire to
mask the scars and pains
we carry.

# When You Wake Up
## April 19, 2021

Don't be afraid to ask yourself
how you are doing today.

If you are not coping,
be honest with yourself
about it.

Your inner honesty with yourself is
a step toward opening up and stepping up.

# Celebrate Them
## April 20, 2021

Someone that follows you through
the road of struggle

is a friend you should never
turn your back on.

And a friend worth celebrating.

# Be Careful Who You Confide In
## April 20, 2021

They will say you can talk to me about it.
But when you talk to them they will laugh
behind your back and
call you names.

Feel the vibe and listen to the energy
before confiding in people,
because some could do you more
harm than good.

# Changes
*April 20, 2021*

I hope your tears will quietly change to
a smile one day.

# The Beauty of Forgiveness
*April 20, 2021*

Sometimes our hurt helps us to
understand how beautiful
it is to forgive.

# Taking Each Day as It Comes
*April 21, 2021*

You can't change yesterday,
but you can do something about tomorrow, today.

So you can look forward to a future and life that
doesn't involve worrying about changing
a past that cannot
be changed.

You can start a better tomorrow, today.
What you do today, often defines tomorrow.

# Finding You
## April 4, 2021

I think you are the kind of person that will make
someone else happy one day,
if you are not doing that already.
Then blessed is the person
who is lucky enough
to find you.

# Attitude
## April 21, 2021

The way you act and think is beautiful.
Please keep being you.

It is you that we love.

# Dear

*April 21, 2021*

Don't worry about them.
I think you are beautiful
anyway.

# The Feelings You Hold
*April 21, 2021*

And yet, I felt deeply sorry for him.

Reasonable people who make unreasonable decisions are often in
a place different from their normal reasonable self
at the time.

Even though it hurts.

Being human is to be compassionate and understanding,
even to those who have done you wrong,
knowingly and unknowingly.

# You Have What You Need
## April 22, 2021

You don't need everything.
You just need to be comfortable with
what you have.

Anything you need but don't have now,
will come to you when the time
is right if it is something you really need.

# It Is Fine

## April 22, 2021

The people who care will show
you understanding and love.

# The Little Things
## April 22, 2021

Sometimes it is the little things you do that
capture the heart of the
one you love.

# Respect Is Not Expensive
April 22, 2021

I saw no respect.
That is why I respectfully walked away.

You can react respectfully too.
It will do your mind and your world good
to walk with your
self-respect.

# Till the End of Time
## April 22, 2021

I'm here.
And I'll always be here with you,
until the end of time.

# Appreciation
## April 22, 2021

You will know the ones who appreciate you
by the way they act and do things.

# How Are You Today?

*April 23, 2021*

All you wanted was for someone to ask
how you are doing today.

And mean it.

# Modern-Day Crucifixion
*April 23, 2021*

To gang up on one person
is a modern day
crucifixion.

# Survivor versus Victim
## April 25, 2021

Even when you are victimized,
refuse to be a victim,
because you are wiser and stronger
than that.
Be a survivor, not a victim.

In time, you will feel empowered
in your own life.

# The Mocking Crew
## April 27, 2021

I can understand why you kept everything
bottled up.
You told them your problems, they laughed and shared them
with others.

You became their laughing stock.

And before you knew it,
they've joined the band wagon of the
mocking crew.

I wish they could see how much damage they have
caused you mentally.

Well, it's not fair, but for now, focus on yourself.
Your well-being is more important to you
than them.
Look after you and be assured that life has
your back.
There is nothing stronger than the power
of life.
Better days are on their way
to you.

All will be well, my friend.

# I Will Be Here with You

*April 27, 2021*

I know how you feel about everything.

You wanted to talk to them.

But you wondered
who cared.

Who is listening?
Who is hearing me?
Who will stand for me?
Who will speak for me?

No one.

So you remained silent.

You are not on your own.

I will be here with you.

# My Hopes for You
## April 27, 2021

I hope you are doing better than
yesterday.
I hope you are calmer with yourself
today.
I hope you are showing some love and care to the
person who is reading this.

I hope that you will stop beating yourself
up over it.

I hope that, regardless of everything,
you will always remember to love the most
important person to you,
which is you.

# The Power within You
## April 30, 2021

The strange thing about mental health is
that it can take control of the life of anyone,
rich or poor.
But we do have the power to control matters
in our lives,
and the inner strength to make it so.

# I Guess What I'm trying to Say Is
May 2, 2021

We all have a role to play in dealing with
mental health issues.
It is not just the responsibility of
doctors, nurses, psychologists,
and other professionals.

We, as individuals
and as members of society,
all have a role to play and something to
contribute too.

Kindness, care, mindfulness, and understanding are
supplements for a broken heart and mind to start healing,
and hopefully start to make sense of their
own lives again.

With a little adjustment in our acts,
and in the way we treat each other,
we can help many others.

# About The Author

**Alexander StPaul Lawani** is a learner whose dream is to use his experiences, knowledge, and understanding of life to help others develop and grow in their own ways. He is the author of the poetry collection, *The Heart that Speaks*.